Genesis 12—25

By faith Abraham and Sarah

by Waldemar Janzen

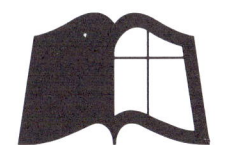

Faith and Life
Bible Studies

Faith and Life Press
Newton, Kansas

By faith Abraham, even though he was past age was enabled to become a father and by faith even Sarah, who was past age, was enabled to bear children because they considered God faithful who had made the promise.
(Hebrews 11:11, New International Version, marginal reading, adapted).

Copyright © 1987 by Faith and Life Press, Newton, Kansas 67114
Printed in the United States of America
Library of Congress Number 86-83035
International Standard Book Number 0-87303-108-3

The publishers gratefully acknowledge the support and encouragement of the Congregational Resources Board of the Conference of Mennonites of Canada in the development of this book.

This publication may not be reproduced, stored in a retrieval system, or transmitted in whole or in part, in any form by any means, electronic, mechanical, photocopying, recording, or otherwise without prior permission of Faith and Life Press. Unless otherwise noted, Scripture quotations in this publication are from the Holy Bible, New International Version. Copyright © 1973, 1978, International Bible Society.

Design by John Hiebert
Printing by Mennonite Press, Inc.

By faith Abraham and Sarah
Table of contents

Introduction. v

SESSION 1. **To the land God showed them**
  (12:1-20). 1
  The city left unbuilt
  The tribe of Terah
  Nation and name in the promise
  Tent pitched and altars built
  Scheming to stay alive

SESSION 2. **Coping with conflict in the new land**
  (13:1—-14:24). 9
  Lot went with them
  Quarreling among the herdsmen
  All the land that you see
  Lot and his family as prisoners of war
  Abraham and his band to the rescue
  Abraham meets the kings

SESSION 3. **Sometimes hard to live by faith**
  (15:1—17:27) 16
  Faith gets special credit
  Day of the covenant
  Hagar in place of the promise
  Seen by God at the spring
  Covenant cut in flesh

SESSION 4. **When God paid a visit**
(18:1—19:38) 23
Still no land and no son!
Date set for that child
Daring to plead for Sodom
Welcome guests in Lot's house
Fast exit from the burning city
Reflections in the dense smoke rising
Kinfolk for the future Israelites

SESSION 5. **God brought laughter to their family**
(20:1—21:34) 34
Sarah as sister once again
The promised son is born!
The promise includes Ishmael, too
An old treaty about water rights

SESSION 6. **The promised son restored**
(22:1-24) 44
Sent to sacrifice on Moriah
Obedience to bless all nations
Twelve cousins in Nahor's house

SESSION 7. **Staking a claim on the promised land**
(23:1-20) 52
Sarah's death and Abraham's grief
For a burial cave four hundred shekels
Deeded to Abraham in the presence of the Hittites

SESSION 8. **Finding a bride for the promised son**
(24:1—25:18) 59
God leads a final time
Full years of faith

Introduction

Abraham and Sarah, as we will come to know them, had no special qualities that made them fit to become the founders of a great nation and world religion except one: faith in the promises of God. They gave up much and risked even more to claim the blessings for which they longed. In ways that they did not expect, God put them to the test. Their grasp on their faith was not always steady, but even when they failed, God did not reject them. In the end, their hope was rewarded and the lives of all they touched were blessed. So firm was their commitment that as we reach out to them across the centuries, we feel our lives being enriched by their witness.

This study guide offers the user a simple and straightforward way to study Genesis. The study process is designed to encourage a careful reading of the text and an application of its teaching to our time. The study guide can be used on an individual basis or in group Bible study.

The eight sessions in this book will guide you step-by-step through this section of Genesis. In order to gain most from this study, follow the steps suggested below.

First, work through the study guide by yourself. Read through the assigned Bible passage several times, watching for special details, as well as for key words and ideas.

In getting acquainted with the passage, consider these questions:

* Why did the authors write these words?
* What did the writers want to share?
* Why is this message important?
* What meaning do these words have for us today?

If you are working through this book with a group, write down your own answers to the questions before meeting with others. The more each person prepares ahead of time, the more fruitful your group study and discussion can be.

Encourage everyone in the group to take part. Be flexible and feel free to use this guide in whatever way benefits you and your group most.

The Bible text used in preparing this study has been the New International Version (NIV).

May this book and your study of Genesis help you to fix your "eyes on Jesus, the author and perfecter of our faith" (Heb. 12:2).

Session 1. To the land God showed them
Genesis 12

Here, in Genesis 12, we read of a new beginning. After Adam and Eve's first disobedience (Gen. 3), the gulf between God and the estranged children of God deepened. The lowest point of that rift was reached in the events at the Tower of Babel (Gen. 11:1-9). There human beings banded together to make a name for themselves, apart from their Creator. God frustrated that attempt by breaking up the plot and scattering "them over the face of the whole earth" (v. 9). We will study that story as a backdrop to the call of Abraham (Abram).

A second passage we need as background is Abraham's family tree (Gen. 11:26-32). It shows Abraham and Sarah (Sarai) and their family to be part of the scattered humanity, a splinter eventually lodged somewhere. "But when they came to Haran, they settled there" (11:31).

A note of hopelessness comes from the comment about the mother of the clan, "Now Sarai was barren; she had no children" (11:30).

In Genesis 12, we are told how God reached into the mass of scattered and settled humans to take out one man and one woman and their family to make a new start. This begins the story of the people of God, a people commissioned to infuse the world with the ways of God; to establish God's kingdom. Let's now look at these events more closely.

2 / BY FAITH ABRAHAM AND SARAH

The city left unbuilt: 11:1-9
This passage shows the human urge to seek identity and security without God.

1. What gave confidence to the Tower builders?

2. What did they want to gain for themselves?

3. What underlying fear drove them?

4. What was the result of their efforts?

5. Compare the outcome of this story with that of Adam and Eve's fall (Gen. 3:24) and of Cain's murdering Abel (Gen. 4:11, 14, 16). What do land, home, rest and departure, wandering, homelessness have to do with sin?

6. Do you recognize some of the traits or marks of the Tower builders in yourself or in other people? If so, list them.

_____
_____
_____

7. Do you recognize some of these traits in the world today? What Towers of Babel are being built? With what results?

_____
_____
_____
_____

The tribe of Terah: 11:26-32
This section outlines Abraham's family background.

1. Draw the family tree given in this passage in the space below.

4 / BY FAITH ABRAHAM AND SARAH

2. Why did God call Abraham, and not someone else? What special qualifications or gifts did Abraham and Sarah have to become the parents of God's people?

_____

_____

3. Check other "call stories" and observe what kinds of people God calls to special service:

Moses: Exodus 2:11-14; 3:10-13

_____

Gideon: Judges 6:11-15

_____

Samuel: 1 Samuel 3:1-20

_____

David: 1 Samuel 16:1-13

_____

Isaiah: Isaiah 6:1-8

_____

Jeremiah: Jeremiah 1:4-10

_____

Peter (Simon): Mark 1:16-18

_____

Paul (Saul): Acts 8:1-3; 9:1-4

_____

Nation and name in the promise: 12:1-3
This is the heart of God's call. It contains a command and a promise.

1. What are the two things Abraham is to do? (See v. 1.)

_____

_____

2. Contrast this verse with Genesis 11:4. How does the command of God to Abraham differ from the intention of the Tower builders?

_____
_____

3. List the six elements of God's promise, each introduced with the words "I will":

_____
_____
_____
_____
_____

4. Some of these statements overlap. What are the two chief items promised, as summarized in verse 7?

_____
_____

Tent pitched and altars built: 12:4-9
Here we observe Abraham's response and its immediate consequence: he and his family become wanderers.

1. What did Abraham do?

_____
_____

2. We do not find out how Abraham felt inside. What might be the reason(s) for the story's silence on this?

3. How is Abraham's moving from one place to another different from Cain (Gen. 4:11, 14, 16) or the scattered Tower builders (Gen. 11:9)?

4. What do we learn here about Abraham's relationship to God?

Scheming to stay alive: 12:10-20
On the surface, this is an excerpt from the ups and downs of ancient, unsettled, wandering groups, always in search of a means just to stay alive, often threatened, needing to use all their cunning to survive, and sometimes to prosper. However, on a deeper level we discover here how God leads his people.

1. This story is closely related to two others, one about Abraham (Gen. 20) and one about Isaac (Gen. 26). Read them and note your observations below. (We will explore the connections between these three events in Session 5 when chapter 20 will be studied.)

2. Why was Abraham afraid that the Egyptians would kill him if they knew that Sarah was his wife?

3. Pharaoh was about to commit adultery without knowing it. We do not know how he found out that Sarah was a married woman. In a similar situation (Gen. 20:3), God warned the king. How might the story have ended if Sarah had actually become Pharaoh's wife?

4. What purpose does the telling of this incident serve at this point in Abraham's and Sarah's life? What does it tell us about Abraham?

5. What does this incident tell us about God's intention for Abraham and Sarah?

As I look back

As I look back, I see the story of a great and surprising new act of God. Humankind had tried to establish its security and identity by banding together in large numbers and making a name for itself by its inventiveness and ability to do great things. God, however, vetoed this effort.

Instead, God called one man and his family, marked by no special qualifications, to leave exactly those securities which the Tower builders had sought, and to set out into the unknown. They would go, however, with the promise that God would give to them what the Tower builders had sought: a name, a nation, a land, and blessing.

Abraham and Sarah followed the call in perfect faith (trust), taking upon themselves a life of insecurity, yet a life guided by God's presence and promise. Would God keep that promise? In the land to which they were led they experienced famine, rather than blessing. Having to seek help in Egypt, Abraham resorted to a lie in the face of danger, rather than to trust in God. Would God reject him now? No. Through God's leading, Sarah was preserved from Pharaoh to become the mother of Israel. God had cleared the way for fulfilling the promise.

Session 2. Coping with conflict in the new land
Genesis 13—14

These two chapters present two rather different stories, but are tied together by Abraham's concern for Lot, a theme that will be continued in chapters 18—19.

Chapter 13 deals with conflict over land. It shows Abraham as the model, one who gives up his own interests in favor of his rival. Lot, on the other hand, acts in typical human fashion, grabbing for the best he can get.

Chapter 14 shows Lot caught in a whirl of politics and warfare (14:1-12). Abraham rescues him from the attacking enemies (14:13-16), but refuses to use the occasion for self-enrichment (14:17-24).

Lot went with them: 13:1-4
This passage continues the description of Abraham's wandering life in Canaan begun in 12:4-9. The detour to Egypt is over.

1. Underline the places to which Abraham moved, according to 12:4-9 and 13:1-4, on the map on page 10. [Add these names to the map: Haran, over 300 miles northeast of Damascus; Moreh, a site near Shechem; and Ai, near Bethel. Canaan was the former name for the land later occupied by the kingdoms of Judah and Israel.]

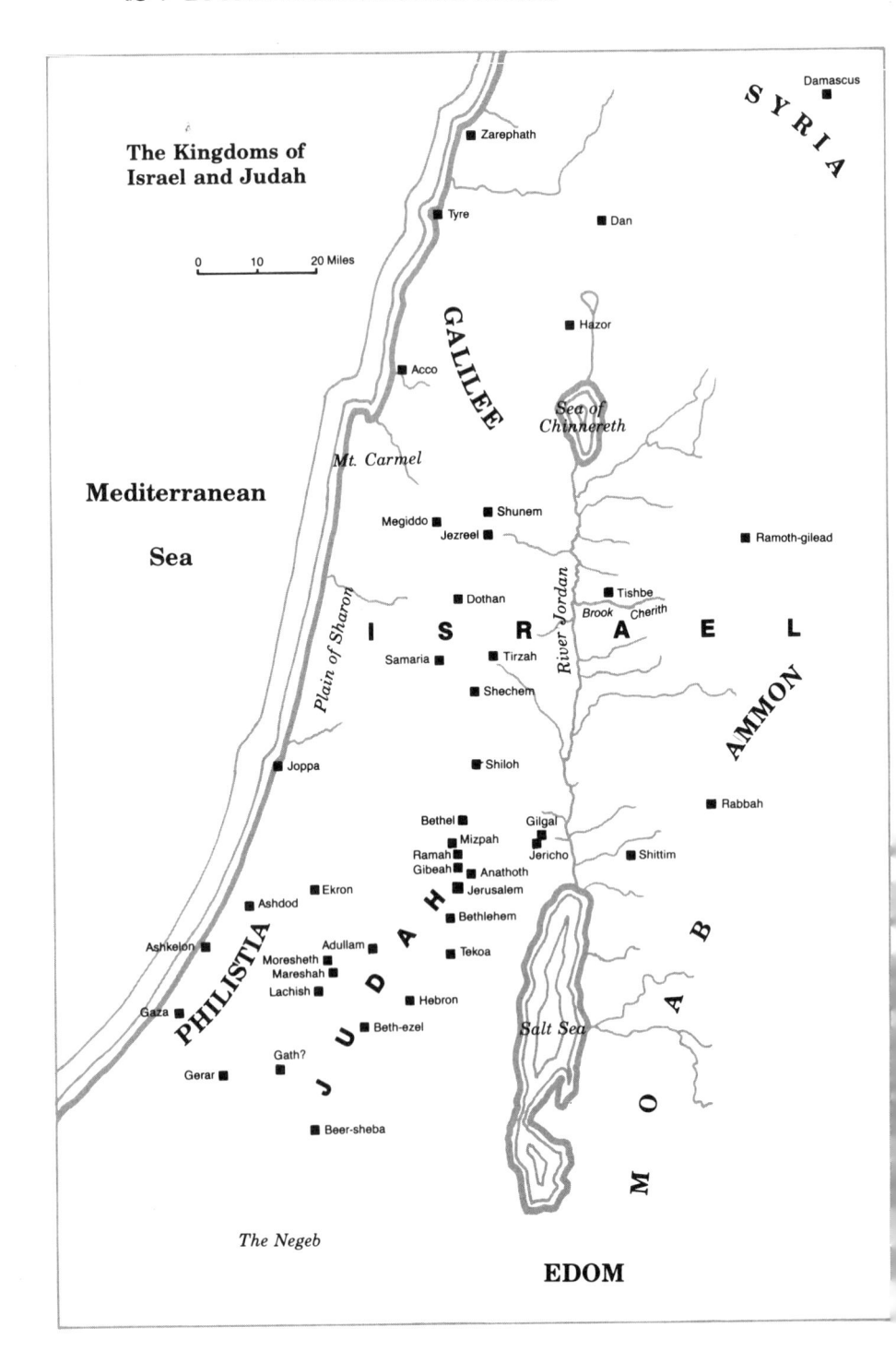

10 / BY FAITH ABRAHAM AND SARAH

2. Which part of God's promise ("I will," 12:2-3) is beginning to be fulfilled, as Abraham's wealth shows?

Quarreling among the herdsmen: 13: 5-13
This section presents a conflict over land and the peaceful resolution of the dispute.

1. Often we picture Abraham and his family as consisting of a few people, with a few tents, flocks, and herds. How could there be a conflict over land in a sparsely settled area? How many persons may have made up Abraham's clan? Read 14:14.

2. How would you describe the difference between the Abraham we saw in 12:10-20 and the one who risks his interests here?

3. God had promised that Abraham's descendants would possess "this land" (12:7; compare 12:1). How do you feel about Abraham's action in offering Lot first choice? Does he not throw God's promise to the winds by doing this? Explain.

12 / BY FAITH ABRAHAM AND SARAH

4. State the principle expressed by Abraham (v. 9) in your own words.

_____

_____

5. State an experience from history, or from your own life, that illustrates such an approach.

_____

_____

6. Where and how did Jesus preach and live out that principle?

_____

_____

7. Locate and underline the place names in verses 10-13 and verse 18 on the map. [Add these names to the map: Zoar, near the southern end of the Salt (or, Dead) Sea; Mamre, near Hebron. Sites for Sodom and Gomorrah are unknown, but may have been on land now covered by the southernmost part of the Dead Sea.]

All the land that you see: 13:14-18
The original promise (12:1-3, 7) is repeated to Abraham once again.

1. Why is the promise repeated at this point in the story?

_____

_____

2. *The promise repeated.* Start a list of passages repeating the promise of land and/or descendants (Gen. 12:1-3)

on the lines below. (Add entries here as you discover them in your study during future sessions.)

_____ _____

_____ _____

_____ _____

_____ _____

Lot and his family as prisoners of war: 14:1-12
The ancient world, like ours, was torn by warfare. Lot and his family were drawn into it by association.

The text does not make it clear whether Lot's involvement in this catastrophe was a punishment for his choice in 13:10-11. What do you think and why?

_____

_____

_____

Abraham and his band to the rescue: 14:13-17
To rescue Lot and his family, Abraham engaged in the only warlike action we know of him.

1. Find Dan and Damascus on your map on page 10.
2. Recall 13:5-13 and page ahead to 21:22-32 for instances that show Abraham as resorting to peaceful means of conflict resolution. What are these means?

_____

_____

_____

Abraham meets the kings: 14:18-24
The returning Abraham had an unexpected encounter with Melchizedek, king of Salem. Then he reached a part-

ing agreement with the king of Sodom, whom he had rescued for Lot's sake.

1. By what two actions did Melchizedek honor Abraham?

_____

_____

2. What are the two titles of the God of Melchizedek, whom Abraham identified as his own God also?

_____

_____

3. Abraham's 318 men (v. 14) were a comparatively small force. How is his victory over several kings explained?

_____

_____

_____

4. Later in the biblical story, the kings of David's line were apparently considered priests "in the order of Melchizedek." Read Psalm 110:4.

5. The title "The Lord God Most High, Creator of heaven and earth" (v. 22), or some part of it, was used frequently in the psalms, and therefore in the later temple worship. Look up Psalms 115:15; 121:2; 124:8; 134:3; 146:6.

6. In the Letter to the Hebrews, Christ is compared to Melchizedek (5:6-10; 6:20; 7:1-28). List the characteristics of Melchizedek, as given in Hebrews 7:1-10, that made him greater than Abraham, and therefore worthy to be a model of Christ.

_____

_____

_____

7. Why did Abraham not want to accept anything from the king of Sodom? What did he want to avoid being accused of?

_____

_____

8. The text does not say it, but we know by now from what source Abraham expected his blessings.

As I look back

Looking back over chapters 13—14, I am impressed with the mystery of God's leading. Abraham risked his own interests by yielding to Lot's wishes. Lot chose the best land. In a sense, he grasped for the fulfillment of God's promise and seemed to have it in hand. But what seemed secure possession, embroiled him in conflict, danger, and loss.

Abraham, on the other hand, received a renewed promise that the land would belong to him and his descendants, just at the point where he let go of it (compare Jesus' word in Matt. 16:25). The faith or trust in God that made Abraham go out into the unknown (12:4) shines here again, after it had been darkened momentarily by his attempt at cunning self-preservation (12:10-20).

Session 3. Sometimes hard to live by faith
Genesis 15—17

In this three-chapter section, the first and the third (15 and 17) tell of how God repeated his promise to Abraham and reassured him of it in several ways. In both chapters, Abraham is asked to perform a ritual. In chapter 15, it is a rather strange sacrifice. In chapter 17, it is the circumcision of all males in his household. Each of these ritual acts is to confirm the covenant between God and Abraham.

In chapter 16, we read how this Abraham, who obediently expressed his allegiance to God in the two covenant ceremonies, agreed to a plan devised by Sarah to hasten the fulfillment of God's promise. According to the customs of the time, Sarah would give her servant Hagar as a substitute wife to Abraham. Hagar's child (or children) would then be the beginning of the fulfillment of God's promise, namely, that Abraham would be the father of a great nation. Immediately, this attempt to help God along leads to strife, injustice, and complication, but it shows, in a beautiful way, how God's grace and blessing are not limited to the main characters of the Bible: they overflow to a lowly foreign servant girl. The story of Hagar and Ishmael will be continued in chapter 21.

Faith gets special credit: 15:1-6
Here Abraham's doubt in God's promise is overcome by God's renewed assurance.

1. Fear or awe is a typical human reaction to an appearance (revelation) of God. With what words does God overcome this fear in the case of

Abraham (15:1) _____

Hagar (21:17) _____

Isaac (26:24) _____

Mary (Luke 1:30) _____

Paul (Acts 27:24) _____

2. What drove Abraham's doubts away and made him believe again (v. 6)?

_____

_____

_____

3. Verse 6 is the beginning of the theme of "justification by faith" in the Bible. Write out these verses and compare them with Gen. 15:6:

Habakkuk 2:4 _____

_____

_____

Romans 1:17 _____

_____

_____

4. Read the Apostle Paul's interpretation of the meaning of Abraham's kind of faith, in Romans 4:1-5.

Day of the covenant: 15:7-21

God, who had just reassured Abraham that he would have a son, now reassures him that he will possess the land.

1. What are the three subdivisions of this passage?

a) Verses (ceremony) _____

b) Verses (dream) _____

c) Verses (ceremony) _____

2. The word *covenant* is introduced into the Abraham story for the first time here (v. 18). Read Jeremiah 34:18-20, where a somewhat similar convenant ceremony is mentioned. Does that passage suggest a possible meaning for walking between animals cut in half? What is it?

_____

_____

_____

3. Why might God have given Abraham the dream wedged between the two parts of the covenant ceremony?

_____

_____

_____

4. Enter the passage in chapter 15 that reaffirms God's promise of land and descendants, in your list on page 13.

Hagar in place of the promise: 16:1-6
Sarah being barren (11:30; 15:2) gives Abraham a substitute wife in the person of her servant Hagar. Complications result.

1. What may have moved Sarah to do what she did?

_____

_____

_____

2. Why did Hagar, when she was pregnant, despise Sarah?

_____

3. Read 1 Samuel 1:1-11. How did Hannah handle a similar situation?

4. How are the events in this passage like those in Genesis 12:10-20 (other than the reference to Egyptians)?

Seen by God at the spring: 16:7-15

Hagar, who has been mistreated by Sarah and has fled, is confronted by the angel of the Lord, given a promise, and sent back to Sarah. There she gives birth to Ishmael.

1. What was Hagar's solution to her problem (v. 6)?

2. What was God's solution (vv. 9-10)?

3. What did God promise to Hagar (vv. 10-12)?

4. What lesson did Hagar learn (v. 13)?

5. What in this passage makes it proper to call it "a miniature gospel to the Gentiles?"

6. Can you think of a situation, where you tried to deal with a problem as Hagar did, that is, by running away? What does Hagar's experience tell you?

7. If you wish to complete your reading of Hagar's story, turn to Genesis 21:8-21.

Covenant cut in flesh: 17:1-27
Like chapter 15, this chapter deals with God's covenant with Abraham. God again affirms the promise and binds the covenant to two special acts: name changing and circumcision.

1. Covenant is a partnership. God's part will be the fulfilling of the promise of descendants and land. What is Abraham's part (vv. 1, 10)?

2. A name change in the Bible always points to a life-changing new beginning. After some years of living by God's promise (even though with doubts and failings), Abraham and Sarah are now in a formal way made covenant partners with God by receiving new names (vv. 3-8, 15-16). Can you recall other biblical characters who were renamed? List them:

_____

_____

Check your memory against these passages: Gen. 32:28; John 1:42; Acts 13:9; compare Exod. 3:13-15, 6:2-3.

4. Check the footnotes in the New International Version for the meanings of these names:

Abram means _____

Abraham means _____

Sarah means _____

Isaac means _____

5. Circumcision is called a "sign of the covenant" (v. 11). What was the sign of God's covenant with Noah (Gen. 9:12-16)?

_____

6. List some ways in which the meanings of circumcision are like the meanings of baptism. Also list ways in which they are different.

_____

_____

_____

7. Look back over chapter 17 and enter the passages reaffirming God's promise on your list on page 13.

As I look back
Looking back, I become ever more aware that patience is an important part of faith. Abraham chafes under the

insecurity of living with a verbal promise; to be sure, the verbal promise is of God, but still only a word. He longs to see and experience its fulfillment (15:2-3, 8). God overcomes his frustration by pointing to the stars and saying, as it were, "If I can make all of these, should I not be able to give you children and children's children?" Abraham accepts the assurance and is ready to live by faith again.

A covenant ceremony (vv. 9-21) adds to the realism of the promise, as the Lord's Supper, for example, confirms our faith in our Lord who gave his body and blood for us.

But the next chapter shows Abraham and Sarah impatient again, ready to hurry God along (16:1-6).

Chapter 17 binds Abraham and Sarah to God through new symbols: new names and a sign on the body (circumcision) marking Abraham and his household as members in a covenant with God. Nevertheless, the burden of uncertainty breaks through in this chapter also (v. 18).

The story of Hagar in chapter 16 (continued in chapter 21) is especially dear to me. I called it a "miniature gospel to the Gentiles." We see that God's concern goes beyond the chosen family. God's grace extends to a Gentile, a woman, a servant. Note also the simplicity, directness, and beauty of 16:7-13. This passage, together with the repeated promise to Ishmael (17:20), shows that God had by no means lost interest in the rest of the world when God singled out Abraham to establish a special people as his instrument in the world (12:1-3). And, just as in the New Testament, it was God who graciously took the first step to save a confused runaway slave girl who did not think of praying to him. (John 3:16 tells us that God acts first to save us.)

Session 4. When God paid a visit
Genesis 18—19

These chapters are held together by the theme of the visit of the three men. The men come with a two-fold task: (1) For Abraham, they bring the promise that the long-expected son will be born within a year (18:1-15). (2) For Sodom and Gomorrah, they bring judgment.

Each chapter is introduced by an arrival scene, in which the three/two men are greeted with unreserved hospitality by Abraham (18:1-8) and Lot (19:1-9), respectively. Then they set about to carry out the tasks for which they have come (18:9-15 and 19:10-26).

Between the two visits stands the story of Abraham's intercession for the cities of Sodom and Gomorrah (18:16-33).

Finally, two sequels to the visit are appended: Abraham realizes that the two cities have been destroyed. He cannot know that his intercession has led to the preservation of Lot and his family, but the storyteller includes that fact (19:27-29). Then, the story concludes with a postscript that identifies Lot as the father of two peoples, the Moabites and the Ammonites (19:30-38).

Still no land and no son! 18:1-8
Abraham sat in front of his tent, a symbol of the wandering, unsettled life. Sarah was busy inside, aged and childless. Then guests arrived. That brought excitement and calls to duty.

24 / BY FAITH ABRAHAM AND SARAH

1. Locate Mamre on the map, page 10. When had Abraham been there before? What had he done there (13:18)?

2. Hospitality was one of the most highly valued virtues in biblical times. Without the public services we know (transportation, hotels, stores, police protection), people were dependent on each other. List at least eight expressions and acts of hospitality on Abraham's part.

3. Note especially two customs that became important elsewhere in the Bible:

(1) Foot washing: read John 13:1-17.

(2) Selecting a choice animal to slaughter for the guests: read 2 Sam. 12:1-4 and Luke 15:23, 27.

4. Hospitality should still be high on our list of Christian virtues. Paul emphasizes it (Rom. 12:13). Recall some instances where you enjoyed unexpected hospitality from strangers.

Date set for that child: 18:9-15

The purpose of the visit is to make the promise of descendants, repeated so often already, precise and close at hand. In one year, Sarah will have borne a son. But Abraham and Sarah have become accustomed to their childlessness by now. They are not receptive to the promise. Sarah can only laugh.

1. It is clear that Abraham receives a visit from God. But God is not a man. Yet God reveals himself in human form, supremely in Jesus Christ. Our story deliberately starts with a human visit from *three* men. Gradually, the one voice of God emerges. But God is deliberately hidden among his companions. Write down the words that apply to the visitor(s) (he, Lord, lord, etc.).

18:15	_____	18:22	_____
18:33	_____	19:1	_____
19:2	_____	19:8	_____
19:10	_____	19:15	_____
19:16	_____	19:16	_____
19:18	_____	19:21	_____

2. Until verse 8, Abraham had acted; now the men take over. Verse 10 (first half) states the purpose of the visit. Sarah's response is disbelief; she laughs. The verb *laugh* occurs four times in verses 12-15. Write out the brief sentences in which it occurs. This will give you the gist of the dialogue.

a) _____

b) _____

c) _____

d) _____

3. What reason is given by the Lord for insisting that Sarah could believe (v. 14)?

4. How does Jesus express the same truth?
Mark 10:27

Mark 14:36

5. In chapter 17:17-19, Abraham also laughed in disbelief. God provided a way to remind them continually, after the birth of their son, of this their unbelief, and of the fact that God had indeed kept his promise. What was it? (Check 17:19 and the NIV footnote to that verse.)

6. Note how 18:1-15 ends in a stalemate (v. 15). Sarah denies her laughter, but the Lord has the last word. How did Zechariah react when a son was promised to him (Luke 1:18)?

How did Mary respond to a similar promise (Luke 1:38)?

Daring to plead for Sodom: 18:16-33
The visit concluded with a farewell. Abraham accompanied his guests for a stretch. Then they lingered in conver-

sation. Eventually two of the men went (v. 22), and finally the Lord also left (v. 33).

Into such a common parting procedure the story has skillfully woven a remarkable self-disclosure of God (vv. 17-21) and an equally remarkable intercession by Abraham, for Sodom and Gomorrah.

1. The setting is near Mamre. Sodom and Gomorrah are thought to have been located in the area now covered by the southern part of the Dead Sea. Zoar, where Lot found refuge, is in that vicinity. Locate these places on the map, page 10.

2. Verses 17-21 express the intimacy of God's relationship to Abraham. Summarize God's intentions for Abraham in calling him, as given in this passage.

_____

_____

_____

3. How was God's will for Abraham summarized in 17:1?

_____

_____

_____

4. State Abraham's plea for Sodom (vv. 23-25) in your own words.

_____

_____

_____

5. Abraham took amazing liberty to argue with God, but we do not find him at all irreverent. List some of the expressions he used that show his respect and humility.

_____

6. Surely we are not dealing here with a numbers game, but with the character of God and of Abraham. What qualities does Abraham assume God to have?

7. What qualities of Abraham emerge in this story?

8. Do you think that a Christian would see God differently than Abraham did, and that a Christian ought to pray differently to God, and for sinful people, than Abraham did? In other words, are we ahead of Abraham, in this scene, in any way?

Welcome guests in Lot's house: 19:1-9
Like the last chapter, this one begins with a welcoming scene. Lot's hospitality fully matches Abraham's. It goes beyond Abraham's in taking risks by protecting the strangers against the hostile townspeople.

1. List at least six statements and/or acts of Lot showing his hospitality (vv. 1-3).

2. The townsmen threaten Lot's guests with violent homosexual assault. No reason is given, but their action is in keeping with the report of 18:20-21. Lot's offer to give them his two daughters instead of his guests is abhorrent to us, but it highlights the sacredness of hospitality. Write out Lot's reason (end of v. 8).

3. Psalm 23:5 uses an image showing God as the ideal host in whose house the guests are safe. Write it out:

Fast exit from the burning city: 19:10-26

While Lot had been the chief actor up to this point, his two visitors took charge now. They led Lot and his family to safety and left Sodom and Gomorrah to their judgment.

1. List at least six actions and orders of the two men/angels (vv. 10-17).

30 / BY FAITH ABRAHAM AND SARAH

2. List all the explanatory clauses (introduced by "so that," "that," "or," "because," "for"):

_____

_____

_____

3. The actions/orders and explanations just listed give the passage a mood of great urgency and seriousness. What else in the passage creates that mood?

_____

_____

_____

4. What is taken for granted in these verses (10-17) about the number of righteous people (18:32) in Sodom and Gomorrah, even though nothing is said directly?

_____

_____

_____

5. The brief reference to the unbelief of Lot's sons-in-law stands in contrast to Lot's willing cooperation with the messengers of God. It underscores once again the difference between Lot and the people among whom he is an alien (v. 9), even though he calls them politely *my friends* (v. 6; literally, *my brothers*). Probably Lot's daughters (virgins, v. 8) were only engaged to these men, but engagement was a firm commitment, not a time of testing. Therefore the men could already be called sons-in-law.

6. The visitors took charge of Lot's escape, but in vv. 18-22, Lot expresses the wish to go to Zoar. Why is he given permission to do so?

_____

_____

7. Verses 23-26 describe the destruction of Sodom and Gomorrah. Lot's wife disobeyed the command not to look around (v. 17) and "she became a pillar of salt" (v. 26). Why might this incident be told? What message does it contain?

Reflections in the dense smoke rising: 19:27-29
Two reflective postscripts about the survivors follow the destruction. We see Abraham, who had pleaded for the sinful cities, as he wordlessly watches the smoke that allows for only one conclusion (vv. 27-28). What he cannot see right away is that his intercession has had some effect anyway (v. 29). These verses invite us to look back and raise several far-reaching questions for thought and discussion.

1. Do you see a connection between Lot's experiences just described and his choice of the good land in chapter 13:10-11? What seems to be the purpose of the whole Lot-theme within the Abraham story anyway?

2. Abraham's plea for Sodom and Gomorrah (18:16-33) is the first prayer for forgiveness (mercy) in the Bible, and it is a prayer, not for the one who prays, but for someone else! What do our two chapters teach about intercessory prayer?

Kinfolk for the future Israelites: 19:30-38
Lot's daughters, having no husbands, tricked their father into making them pregnant. To us that sounds like shocking incest, and some censure may indeed be implied here. However, the daughters' motivation, "so we can preserve our family line" (v. 34), would have sounded noble to people then. The incest involved may have been seen as an emergency means to a desirable end.

There is another important point. All our stories highlight the main characters, but as we saw in the case of Abraham (Gen. 14:14), these were not lonely individuals, but represented sizable clans. Our passage under discussion characterizes two peoples, the Moabites and the Ammonites. They are the true descendants of Lot, the nephew of Abraham, rather than of mixed origin. Therefore they are also genuine kinsmen to the later Israelites.

As I look back
As I look back over chapters 18 and 19, I am, first of all, delighted by a fascinating story. A visit by three strange wayfarers gradually and mysteriously evolves into a revelation of God. That can be the reward of hospitality.

Then, a lingering farewell turns into an intense and compassionate pleading for a relative and friend who has not always been easy to get along with.

And, finally, the one who went to all lengths to save his guests was himself wonderfully rescued by their superhuman power and was able to start a new life in a new setting.

As I look back, I am also puzzled. Can one speak in such human ways about God? Does God really walk the streets to come and see whether rumors of certain cities are true? Do we have here ancient and primitive views of God?

Then I remind myself that all speaking of God has to be in human language for our sake. The Old Testament is well aware that God transcends all human ways of presenting him (1 Kings 8:27-30). It is God's grace to address us humans in our language, in the stories of the Old Testament, in the history of Israel, and in the human form of Jesus Christ.

As I look back, I am also aroused to awe. God's determination, both to fulfill his promise and to bring judgment of sin, emerges so forcefully. Sarah's laugh cannot halt God's promise, nor the self-assurance of the Sodomites God's judgment. Will you and I live by grace to escape the judgment?

Session 5. God brought laughter to their family

Genesis 20—21

Our next section, consisting of two chapters, begins and ends with an encounter between Abraham and Abimelech (20:1-17 and 21:22-34). Abraham, chief of a wandering clan, and Abimelech, king of the city-state of Gerar, met in a variety of disputes such as intermarriage and claims to wells. Disputes arose and were resolved again. That has always been the state of affairs where wandering shepherds and settled farmers meet. (Compare Cain and Abel, Gen. 4.)

Into the midst of this ongoing routine, our story places the birth of Isaac (21:1-7). Finally, after years and years of waiting, God's promise was being fulfilled. The story is almost too brief and too sober for our taste, yet its importance must not be missed. God's plan has reached a milestone.

The birth of the promised son raises a problem, however: What about the other son, Ishmael? That is the problem which occurs whenever we speak of election. Does the election of one mean the rejection of another? The answer is both yes and no. Isaac is chosen for God's special purposes, but Ishmael is also loved and blessed (21:8-21).

Sarah as sister once again: 20:1-17
In a way similar to 12:10-20, Abraham presented Sarah as his sister. Abimelech took her into his house, expecting

to marry her. The Lord warned him in a dream. Abimelech scolded Abraham and returned Sarah, together with gifts to make good any wrong he might have done unwittingly. In spite of his deceit, Abraham emerged from the episode the better for it, but Abimelech and his people were also preserved by God.

1. Follow Abraham's movements by marking the place names of verse 1 on the map, page 10. [Kadesh and Shur are regions in the Sinai desert, south of the Negev (or, Negeb).]

   2. Outline the chapter into the following sections:

a) Introduction of problem, vv. _____

b) Conversation between God and Abimelech, vv. _____

c) Conversation of Abimelech and Abraham, vv. _____

d) Resolution of conflict, vv. _____ _____

   3. The conversation between God and Abimelech is much like a lawsuit. Summarize the following in your own words:

a) Of what does God accuse Abimelech?

_____

_____

b) What is Abimelech's defense?

_____

_____

c) What is God's judgment?

_____

_____

   4. Abimelech's conversation with Abraham also contains accusation and defense. Summarize these, again in your own words.

36 / BY FAITH ABRAHAM AND SARAH

a) Abimelech accuses Abraham:

b) Abraham's excuse:

5. Several things are done to set the situation right.
a) What does Abimelech do?

b) What does Abraham do?

c) What does God do?

6. Having studied the story, we can go on to several questions raised by it. The first has to do with character. How would you describe Abraham's character here?

7. Our sympathies probably lie with Abimelech. So do those of God who absolved Abimelech from intentional sin (v. 6). The expression "with a clear conscience" (RSV, better: "in the integrity of your heart") is very similar, in the original Hebrew, to God's demand of Abraham, in 17:1, to be "blameless." Compare also Abimelech's statement in 20:4, to Abraham at his best, in 18:23. Describe the relationship between God and Abimelech.

8. The point of the story is obviously not that Abraham is more righteous than Abimelech. But what is the point of the story, then? (I will give my opinion in the section "As I Look Back.")

9. Why is this incident introduced at this point in the Abraham story? How would the Abraham story be affected if chapter 20 were left out? (Check your interpretation against mine in "As I Look Back.")

10. Abraham presented his wife as his sister in 12:10-20 already. Later in this history, Isaac will present his wife Rebekah to Abimelech of Gerar (!) as his sister (chap. 26). That chapter concludes with a story about the digging of wells and the naming of Beersheba, just as 21:22-34 in our present lesson. What do you make of three stories that are so similar? (Check your interpretation against mine in "As I Look Back.")

The promised son is born! 21:1-7

1. Verse 1 connects directly with 18:10. Look up that verse. Chapters 19-20 have given us the impression that some time has elapsed.

2. Restate the expression "the Lord was gracious to Sarah" in your own words.

3. The age of Abraham (and Sarah) is stressed here, for it underlines God's special intervention. How does the writer to the Hebrews speak of Abraham's age (Heb. 11:11)?

4. We have not given attention so far to the various times when Abraham's and/or Sarah's age was mentioned. Look back and fill in their age(s) at various points in the story.

12:4 Occasion: _____

Age of Abraham: _____

16:16 Occasion: _____

Age of Abraham: _____

17:1 Occasion: _____

Age of Abraham: _____

17:17 Occasion: _____

Age of Sarah: _____

SESSION 5 / 39

Age of Abraham: _____

17:24 Occasion: _____

Age of Abraham: _____

25:7 Occasion: _____

Age of Abraham: _____

23:1 Occasion: _____

Age of Sarah: _____

5. How is Abraham's obedience noted in this passage? See 17:12.

_____

_____

6. The theme of laughter is taken up from 17:17 and 18:9-15. How is Sarah's laughter here (vv. 6-7) different from the laughter in these earlier passages?

_____

_____

Do you recall the meaning of the name Isaac? See 17:19, including the NIV footnote.

_____

7. Christians live by promise and hope, but sometimes God gives us an experience that we recognize as the fulfillment of our hopes and prayers. Such an experience becomes a sign that God is leading us. Can you recall such a sign in your life?

_____

_____

_____

40 / BY FAITH ABRAHAM AND SARAH

The promise includes Ishmael, too: 21:8-21
Sarah, having a son of her own now, perceived Ishmael as a rival. She asked Abraham to expel Hagar and Ishmael. Abraham was reluctant to do so, but God told him to go ahead. That drove Hagar and her child into the desert and to the brink of death. However, God had allowed this only to show them special care, as had been shown earlier (16:7-13).

1. Describe Sarah's attitude to Hagar (16:1-5; 21:8-10).

2. Describe Abraham's attitude to Hagar (16:6; 21:11, 14).

3. Describe God's attitude to Hagar (16:7, 13; 21:17-20).

4. Why did God care for and bless Ishmael? It is interesting to note an answer on several levels:

a) God acts on his own, for reasons not clear to us (16:10-12; 21:12-13).

b) God also responds to Abraham's petition (17:18, 20).

c) God responds in pity to the child's crying (not to Hagar's praying!) (21:17-18).

An old treaty about water rights: 21:22-34
After the birth of Isaac and the concern for the respective

roles of Isaac and Ishmael, we return to the problems and concerns of Abraham's wandering life and, more specifically, to his interaction with Abimelech, king of Gerar. In a dry land, rivalry over water resources can be a major cause of conflict. Abraham and Abimelech solve it peacefully, by means of a treaty.

1. Abimelech expressed Abraham's relationship to God in a classical statement (v. 22). Write it out.

_____

_____

2. What reason does he have to make this statement?

_____

3. What reason does he have for wanting assurance that Abraham will not deal falsely with him and his descendants (v. 23)?

_____

_____

4. Into the general treaty between Abraham and Abimelech, sealed by an oath (v. 24), is woven the story of a special treaty (literally: "covenant") about the possession of a particular well (vv. 25-26, 28-30, 32). By accepting the gift of the lambs (v. 30), Abimelech apparently recognized Abraham's legitimate claim to the disputed well.

5. In Hebrew, *be'er* means well. *Sheba*, according to the NIV footnote to verse 31, can mean:

_____ or _____

What, then, are the two possible meanings of Beersheba?

_____

Underline this important place in Palestine on your map on p. 10.
    6. The reference to the Philistines (v. 32) is an anachronism. The area in which Gerar lay was not occupied by the Philistines until many centuries after Abraham's time.

As I look back.
As I look back, I remind myself of the way in which God's special act, the fulfillment of his promise, occurs right in the midst of the affairs of ordinary life.

I find that my human sympathies in these chapters lie with Abimelech, rather than Abraham (chap. 20), and with Hagar, rather than Sarah (chap. 21). And it seems to me, that God sees it that way, too. That makes me think of the church today, and of the fact that God's chosen people often do not compare well with outsiders (the Abimelechs, Hagars, and Ishmaels of our time). Nevertheless, the church (like Abraham, Sarah, and Isaac) is called to a special task.

But again, this does not mean that God loves the chosen more, or that God does not care for outsiders. God's treatment of Abimelech and Hagar seems particularly understanding and tender in our texts.

As I look back, I am very aware of a feature of the total Abraham story (Gen. 12—25) and, in fact, all of Genesis, that we have not yet discussed. We have treated it as an ongoing, coherently flowing story. But have you not felt frequent abrupt breaks between one section and another? And what about the repetitious "wife is sister" incidents?

Many Bible scholars believe that the story extending from Genesis to Numbers was originally not written as one story, but that it circulated in two or three separate versions, somewhat like the four gospels in the New Testament. These separate accounts were then woven together into one Bible story, but still allowing the different styles or variant ways of telling a particular incident in the original stories to shine through. That has resulted in some bumpiness and repetition of themes in our present text.

One minor illustration of this is the age of Ishmael. In 17:25 he was thirteen years old, but in 21:15-19 he seems to be a small child. Probably the original stories placed the events somewhat differently in time and sequence (as the Gospels often do), and in the final story these minor rough spots were not smoothed out. This adds variety to the picture and does no harm to the message of the story as a whole.

Session 6. The promised son restored

Genesis 22

This chapter could be considered the high point of the Abraham story. It comes as a complete surprise. Reading 21:1-7, we breathed a sigh of relief as the long-promised son was finally born and the tension of waiting was over. Now, in a totally unexpected move, God put the fulfillment of God's own promise in jeopardy, by asking Abraham to sacrifice his own son.

The silent but immediate and unprotesting obedience of Abraham shows his faith at its maturest point. He was ready to place his whole future into God's hands, as he had done in 12:1-4. This time, however, no long story of waiting resulted; God acted immediately to provide a ram as a substitute sacrifice, preserving Isaac and repeating the promise once more. Now Isaac really belonged to Abraham, having been given to him by God for a second time.

A little bit of family history concludes the chapter.

Sent to sacrifice on Moriah: 22:1-12

In this section, God tested Abraham. The test began with God's request to offer Isaac and concluded with the statement that Abraham, being willing to put the life of his son on the altar, had met the test.

1. Twice in this section Abraham is addressed by God. Fill in the verse and the address:

a) Verse: _____ Address: _____

b) Verse: _____ Address: _____
Each time he answers:

a) _____

b) _____

2. Compare two similar incidents of address and response:

Exodus 3:4:

Address: _____

Response: _____

1 Samuel 3:4:

Address: _____

Response: _____

3. Abraham's response shows more than a simple acknowledgment that he has heard. It expresses his readiness to be at God's service. In each instance, a command follows. Write out the main point of the first command:

_____

Write out the main point of the second command:

_____

4. What is the purpose of these two contradictory commands? What verb expresses it in verse 1?

_____

What statement of God gives the reason why the second command could annul the first one?

_____

5. Abraham's feelings are not described, and yet the story is highly charged with emotion. List several words, phrases, and circumstances that contribute to this:

6. Only two brief speeches of Abraham are reported for the three days' journey. The second may be considered Abraham's deepest confession of faith, and the summary of this chapter. Write it out.

7. Does anything in this story remind you of Jesus in Gethsemane (Mark 14:32-42)?

8. The Bible says repeatedly that God tests people. How did God test Israel in the wilderness (Deut. 8:2)?

How did God test Job (Job 1:8-12)?

9. How did Jesus teach us to pray regarding temptation (Matt. 6:13; Luke 11:4)?

But God does not test/tempt us with the desire to bring us to our downfall. Write out 1 Corinthians 10:13.

10. Read Hebrews 11:17-19 as a summary of this section. There, Abraham is moved by faith to do something that runs counter to God's own promise. How could he do that (v. 19)?

How is Abraham's action related to the resurrection from the dead?

Compare Genesis 22:8 with Hebrews 11:19. What common point do these verses make?

Obedience to bless all nations: 22:13-19
Two consequences follow as soon as Abraham had met

God's test. First, God provided an animal as a substitute offering for Isaac (vv. 13-14). Secondly, God renewed the promise that Abraham's descendants would be many and would possess the land (vv. 15-18). A brief statement about the return trip concludes the events begun in 22:1 (v. 19).

1. People in ancient times will have heard something here, and in the whole story, that we could easily miss. Child sacrifice was not common even among the heathen peoples around Israel, but it did occur in exceptional situations and was considered the ultimate sign of devotion to the gods. Pious Israelites must often have asked themselves whether they did not also owe their God this highest gift of loyalty. Some actually did so. Describe briefly the incident of child sacrifice in Judges 11:29-40.

_____

_____

Describe briefly the incident reported in 1 Kings 16:34.

_____

_____

2. What message must our Abraham story (22:1-19) have given to people who wondered whether they owed God the life of their child?

_____

_____

3. In later times, the law made it a rule that Israel should acknowledge God's ownership of all life by redeeming the firstborn of humans and animals through a sacrifice (Exod. 13:13; 34:20; Num. 18:15-18). Another form of

acknowledging God's claim to life, and God's grace in accepting an animal substitute, is the possibility to atone for human sin by animal blood; see especially the sacrifice on the Day of Atonement (Lev. 16).

4. Place names often commemorated events, and in turn, stories of events explained place names and popular sayings. Compare verse 14 with verse 8. What is the phrase central to both?

_____

5. Compare the place naming with similar namings in other passages. Often the NIV footnotes are helpful to explain the connection between the name and the event:

Genesis 11:8-9:

Event: _____

Name: _____

Meaning: _____

Genesis 16:13-14:

Event: _____

Name: _____

Meaning: _____

Genesis 21:31:

Event: _____

Name: _____

Meaning: _____

6. Verses 15-17 are a renewal of God's promise. Why does it come at this point in the story?

_____

_____

_____

7. Note how *angel of the Lord* (v. 15) and *Lord* (v. 16) are really the same. We should think of the expression "angel of the Lord" as a restrained, veiled way of speaking of God as the presence of God becomes known, rather than dwell on the thought of a separate heavenly being.

8. Several expressions in verses 15-18 make contact with earlier passages. Check these and write out the expressions.

Verse 16 (22:12)

_____

Verse 17 (15:5)

_____

Verse 18 (12:3)

_____

9. Verse 18 reminds us very much of God's original promise of blessing on Abraham (12:3), but there is one addition:

_____

Why was that addition absent from 12:3, but can be made now?

_____

_____

10. Enter the repetition of the promise, verses 15-18, on your list on page 13.

11. Verse 19 makes a brief mention of the return trip. Mount Moriah (v. 2) is often identified with the later temple hill. If that is so, it would be right next to Jerusalem. Mark the latter, as well as Beersheba, on your map on page 10.

Twelve cousins in Nahor's house: 22:20-24

Now that Abraham's line has a chance to continue, we are reminded of the network of families and clans from which Abraham came and from which his son Isaac and his grandson Jacob would get their wives. Perhaps this is one of the many reminders that God, through pursuing his special plans with Abraham's family, has not forgotten the other peoples. The reference to Rebekah here is probably made in anticipation of the role she would soon play in Abraham's family (chap. 24).

As I look back

As I look back, I see Abraham encountering a problem of an entirely new sort. Until now he had risked a move into the unknown, coped with famine, negotiated concerning land and water rights, and waited more or less patiently for the fulfillment of God's promise. In all of this, he exhibited trust in God's leading and experienced that God was with him (21:22), even if much patience was needed to maintain hope.

Now suddenly, God no longer seems to be with him, but to meet him as an enemy set to undo what had seemed like his own doing. Had God not promised and then given this son to Abraham? And now God would take him away again?

Here Abraham's faith reached a new maturity; it is a faith not limited to trusting a leading, blessing, and protecting God, but also a God who could step into the way as an adversary. Jacob would meet that God later, too (chap. 32:22-32) and wrest a blessing from him. Job and the psalmists (Ps. 22:1) faced him and did not let go of him. Jesus Christ, more than anyone, reached a point where he was apparently deserted by God (Matt. 27:46). Have you experienced situations where God seems to be your enemy; where God apparently takes away the very blessing which you had received gratefully from God's hand?

But as I look back, I also hear the good news for such situations. As the writer to the Hebrews put it, Isaac was, figuratively speaking, raised from the dead (Heb. 11:17-19), pointing ahead to God's own son, sacrificed and raised again.

Session 7. Staking a claim on the promised land

Genesis 23

This chapter describes how the death of Sarah became the occasion for Abraham to acquire full legal possession of one small piece of that land which God had promised to him and his descendants. Abraham, the landless alien and stranger, gains a foothold in the promised land of Canaan.

Sarah's death and Abraham's grief: 23:1-2
These verses set the stage. They report the death of Sarah and explain why is was necessary for Abraham to buy a piece of land at this time.

1. Sarah died at the age of 127. How many years had passed since the birth of Isaac (17:17, 24; 21:5)?

2. Locate Kiriath Arba on your map on page 10. What was its other, better-known name?

For a burial cave four hundred shekels: 23:3-16
This section, making up the major part of our chapter, describes the bargaining that ended in Abraham's purchase of the field and the cave of Machpelah. In many ways, it is a typical Oriental bargaining scene.

1. In their introductory statements, the two parties show Oriental politeness. How does Abraham introduce himself with all humility?

How do the Hittites honor him in their address?

2. The progression of the bargaining may emerge most clearly if we outline it. Summarize the requests and responses of the two parties:
Abraham's original request:

The Hittites' first response:

Abraham's second, more specific request:

Ephron's reply:

Abraham's response to Ephron:

Ephron's price offer:

___

Ephron probably stated a very high sum, although it is hard to evaluate ancient prices today. What could we expect Abraham to say in reply?

___

Abraham's actual response:

___

3. List some of the forms of polite address that appear in this dialogue and that may strike us as flowery or pompous:

___

___

4. The offer of the Hittites that Abraham should bury Sarah in one of their sepulchers may be an expression of hospitality. Jesus was laid in the tomb of Joseph of Arimathea (Matt. 27:57-60). At the same time, it might show some hesitation to sell land to Abraham.

5. The offer of Ephron to give the field to Abraham is probably a euphemism for sell (see NIV footnote). Some have suggested that, by accepting the land as a gift, Abraham would have become a vassal of Ephron. We do not know the laws of those times well enough to be able to say exactly what the offers of the Hittites and of Ephron meant.

6. How do you interpret Abraham's readiness to pay the full price in strong currency ("according to the weight current among the merchants") without any further bargaining?

Deeded to Abraham in the presence of the Hittites: 23:17-20

These verses restate Abraham's clear legal title to the field and the cave of Machpelah once more, with full detail. They make brief mention of the burial of Sarah.

1. While we discussed the transaction between Abraham and Ephron as a business deal, it is also a legal transaction "in the gate," that is, in court. What features of a court proceeding can you discover in this chapter?

2. The information of verses 17-20 could be drawn up in a legal document containing these items:

Purchaser: _____

Vendor: _____
Description of real estate:

Location of real estate:

56 / BY FAITH ABRAHAM AND SARAH

Dated at: _____

Witnesses: _____

3. Why was it so important to emphasize Abraham's full legal claim to this piece of land?

_____

_____

_____

4. While the story does not mention God and God's leading, it makes an important theological point. Can you state it? (See "As I Look Back" for my way of saying it.)

_____

_____

_____

5. Read Jeremiah 32:1-15, to see another example of a land purchase with a theological meaning. Why did Jeremiah buy a piece of land?

_____

_____

_____

6. Can you see any connection between the outcome of this chapter and the outcome of chapter 22? (I will state my opinion in "As I Look Back.")

_____

_____

_____

7. The cave of Machpelah became the burial plot of the patriarchs. A great monument stands over its traditional site today and is shown to tourists. List the couples buried there, according to Genesis 49:29-32:

Why was Rachel, Jacob's favorite wife, not buried there with him? (See Gen. 35:16-21.)

8. In Hebrews 11:13-16, the writer reflects on the relationship of Abraham and Sarah and their descendants to the land in which they died. How does he characterize it, in spite of the beginning of the fulfillment of God's promise that they would possess the land?

Would the patriarchs themselves have agreed with the writer to the Hebrews?

As I look back

As I look back, I recognize that the story of our chapter needs to be read on at least three levels.

First, it represents a vivid account of the kind of transactions that must have been part of the daily life of wandering peoples, such as the patriarchs, in ancient times. They had to negotiate time and again, in all kinds of matters, with the settled population of the land, as we have observed earlier (12:10-20; 14; 20; 21:22-34).

Secondly, our story, in its simple account of a deal, and without any pious words, makes one of the strongest theological statements in the Book of Genesis. It shows how a land purchase that seems totally human and "everyday-ish" is, for those who can see it, a part of the mysterious but purposeful leading of God. It is the beginning of the fulfillment of the promise that God would give a new land to Abraham and his descendants (12:1-3). In this respect, it links up with chapter 22, where a beginning was made towards the fulfillment of the promise of many descendants. Abraham, who had been promised to become a large nation and possess the whole land of Canaan, had now, shortly before his death, received one son and one plot of land.

That brings us to the third level of our story, the level highlighted by the writer to the Hebrews. God's promises in the Old Covenant were very concrete and realistic: children and land. The people of the Old Covenant received very realistic tokens of beginning fulfillment. Abraham got one son and one plot of land. That was a foretaste of God's goals. It did not yet turn believing into seeing (Heb. 11:1). Centuries later, Israel in Egypt became a great nation (Exod. 1:1-6), and after a long story of wandering, conquered the land in God's strength (Josh. 1—24). But land and descendants were the concrete expression of shalom, fullness of life. That fullness is experienced only in foretaste even by Christians, leaving room for faith, that is, for the ongoing trust in God's leading. All believers remain strangers and pilgrims in this world, with foretaste experiences of fulfillment, to be sure. Only when we have arrived in eternity with God, in "the city with foundations, whose architect and builder is God" (Heb. 11:10), will the life of wandering in faith, by promise, which Abraham began, come to its final destination and rest (Heb. 11:39-40).

Session 8. Finding a bride for the promised son

Genesis 24:1-25:18

This section is the conclusion of Abraham's story. Sarah had already died. Abraham himself was old. He had experienced, to some degree, the fulfillment of God's original promises (12:1-3); God had blessed him. He had received the long-awaited son who was to be his heir. He was almost ready to die.

Only one thing weighed on his mind. Would the work that God had begun through his own life continue through his descendants? The major threat to the fledgling people of God—to use a later biblical term a bit prematurely—would be acculturation—to become lost in the native Canaanite population through intermarriage. To prevent this, Abraham took special precaution to find a wife for Isaac from among his own kinfolk in Mesopotamia.

When that was done, the storyteller briefly fills in a few details about Abraham's second marriage. Then he is ready to report Abraham's death and burial briefly, without pathos, but with deep though restrained emotion.

God leads a final time: 24:1-67
We turn now to the long and detailed, but singularly beautiful and touching account of the servant's mission to find a wife for his master's son. On the surface it is probably a rather typical matchmaking story that reveals

60 / BY FAITH ABRAHAM AND SARAH

many customs of ancient times. On a deeper level, it draws to our attention one final time all the ways of God with Abraham.

1. Verses 1-9 describe the oath Abraham exacts from his chief (or oldest) servant. The name of the servant is not given. Some would identify him with Eliezer of Damascus (15:2). List the two things Abraham made him swear:

a) _____

_____

_____

b) _____

_____

_____

2. Why is Abraham so set against these two possibilities? What would be the consequences of

possibility a? _____

_____

_____

possibility b? _____

_____

_____

3. The ritual of placing the servant's hand under Abraham's thigh (vv. 2, 9; compare 47:29) is one of the many ancient customs reflected in this chapter. Some commentators think that "thigh" is a euphemism (an indirect reference to avoid a direct statement that might be offensive) for genitals. If that were true, the custom would go back to the ancient notion that the genitals, being the organs of procreation of new life, are particularly sacred. The custom would correspond loosely to the modern prac-

tice of placing one's hand on the Bible when swearing an oath in court.

4. Verse 5 reckons with the possibility that the chosen future bride might not consent to a move so far away. This shows that women, even in that patriarchal society, enjoyed more personal freedom of decision than some other Old Testament passages might make us think. As you continue to read the chapter, note further evidence supporting this observation.

Verses 10-21 describe the servant's journey from its outset to his meeting with Rebekah. This section informs us on geography and family relationships, but its core is theological. It shows how surface events, which many might attribute to chance, can become the leading and language of God for those who are sensitive to God's work.

1. The scene at the well outside of town presents an age-old picture, extending from the time of Abraham to the time of Jesus. (Read Gen. 29:1-14, Exod. 2:15-22, and John 4:1-9, 27-30.) What similarities of situation and custom do you see in these stories?

Do you observe a contrast between the Old Testament stories and the New Testament story with respect to the attitude toward women?

2. Rebekah was introduced to us in 22:23 already; in anticipation of her later importance. Find her on the family tree on page 3.

Nahor was Rebekah's _____

Milcah was Rebekah's _____

Bethuel was her _____

Laban was her _____

Abraham was her _____

Isaac was her _____

3. In verse 16, Rebekah is described as

_____ and _____

From her words and actions towards the servant we can also attribute other characteristics to her, such as:

_____

_____

_____

4. So far, we have considered externals. The heart of the story, however, is the sign that the servant asked of God and was granted by God. Read the prayer of the servant again (vv. 12-14). The word *kindness* (RSV: "steadfast love") occurs twice (see also v. 27). It is the Hebrew *hesed*, which is also found in verses 27 and 49, there supported by the word *faithfulness*. It could also be described as "loyalty to a relationship," or "faithfulness in keeping a promise or obligation once assumed," or more popularly, the stick-with-it-no-matter-what quality. In other words, the servant prays that God may continue to the very end in that abiding commitment to Abraham which has marked our whole Abraham story so far. On the human plane, Abraham showed this loyalty, as our present chapter shows. In verse 49, the servant invited Bethuel and

Laban to become partners to this story of loyal relationships by showing kindness and faithfulness to Abraham.

5. Note the delicately drawn picture presented in verses 20-21: The young girl, eager to serve, runs back and forth with her water jar, totally unaware of anything extraordinary. Meanwhile, the old man stands to the side watching her closely, with a growing awareness that the unselfconscious behavior of this girl is nothing less than the answer of God to his prayer.

6. What do you think of such a request to God for a sign? (Compare your reactions to mine, below).

Invited by Laban, (vv. 22-33). This is another hospitality story; compare the hospitality shown to strangers by Abraham (18:1-8) and Lot (19:1-9). While the servant knew by now that his hosts were Abraham's relatives (to whom God had led him), they were unaware of this. Laban simply offered hospitality to a stranger deserving respect, as his rich gifts to Rebekah show. But the normal, even if extra-polite, reception of a guest was interrupted by the servant's sense of urgency about his mission (v. 33).

The matchmaker's story, (vv. 34-49). The earlier part of the chapter is repeated here as the servant tells his story, including the signs of divine leading, to Rebekah's family, adding his request for Rebekah's hand for Isaac.

1. The story is not retold here exactly as in the earlier verses. What purpose do the variations serve?

2. In both parts, reference is made to an angel that would lead the servant (vv. 7 and 40). But then the servant

says that it was *God* who had led him (v. 48). Review our discussion on the use of the term *angel*, above, page 50.

3. Write out the phrases that describe God in this chapter. Of what do they remind us?

Verse 3: _____

_____

Verse 7: _____

_____

Verse 12: _____

_____

Verse 27: _____

_____

Verse 40: _____

_____

Verse 42: _____

_____

Verse 48: _____

_____

Gifts and blessings for the bride, (vv. 50-61). The host family fully accepted the servant's story of God's leading and responded by sending Rebekah along with the servant to become Isaac's wife.

1. Why does the servant not give Rebekah ten more days with her family? Compare his haste in verse 33.

_____

_____

_____

2. Laban, Rebekah's brother, plays a more prominent role in the whole story than her father Bethuel. Probably Bethuel was old, and Laban was the active head of the household.

3. Their farewell blessing is probably a traditional wish for a bride. Read Ruth 4:11-12.

However, as a part of God's story to Abraham, it must be heard with special reference to the promise that God would make Abraham into a great nation (12:1-3).

Verses 62-67 report the meeting and union of Isaac and Rebekah. We wonder why Abraham, who sent the servant on his mission, is not mentioned. It almost appears as if Isaac and Rebekah met accidentally in a field. Perhaps this is so to highlight the nature of God's leading as it is characterized throughout this story: that which looks accidental on the surface is nevertheless the result of God's subtle direction.

1. Identify the meaning of the name of the place (well) Beer Lahai Roi (see 16:7-14).

The name means: _____

2. After the first meeting, the story tells in a few brief sentences that Abraham's wish had been met (vv. 1-9) and that the servant's mission had been successfully completed. Note the order in which verse 67 lists the steps of the union between Isaac and Rebekah:

Isaac _____

and he _____

So she _____

and he _____

What is it in this sequence that surprises a modern reader?

_____

_____

Why does it fit an arranged marriage?

3. Why is the twofold association of Rebekah with Sarah important?

Full years of faith: 25:1-18
The account of the death of Abraham forms the core of this section. It is preceded by a few verses on Abraham's marriage to Keturah.

Verses 1-4 may seem like an unwelcome interruption in the account of how God established a people for himself through Abraham and his line descended through Isaac. But perhaps we are to be kept from isolating Abraham and Isaac as the lonely chosen ones. Their story has its setting in the ancient world, its customs and its peoples. Isaac was not Abraham's only son, just as Jesus was not the only son of Mary and Joseph (Matt. 13:55-56). God's chosen belong in the midst of the rest of humanity and are related to other peoples in many ways. Historically, the list of descendants of Abraham and Keturah undoubtedly characterizes the relationships of various ancient tribes to the Israelites.

Verses 5-6 speak of Abraham's disposition of his property. What distinction is made between Isaac and "the sons of his [Abraham's] concubines"?

Verses 7-11 report Abraham's death and burial.

1. Compare Abraham's age (v. 7) with his age as given for various important events in his life. See Session 5, pages 38-39.

2. Verse 8 describes a "good death" in four positive statements. List them:

_____

_____

_____

3. For comparison, read the characterization of aging by a content old man, Barzillai, who is ready to die (2 Sam. 19:31-37). What does a full life mean to you? How important is life's length? What ingredients must it have?

_____

_____

_____

4. Read Hebrews 11:13-16, to supplement your understanding of fulfillment in Abraham's life. In what sense did it remain unfulfilled?

_____

_____

_____

5. Abraham is buried by Isaac and Ishmael, mentioned as equal partners in this last duty to their father. We too, belong both to the family of faith and to our natural or biological family.

6. The burial place is the cave of Machpelah (see Session 7, on chap. 23). Burial with one's family was important to the people of the Old Testament. (Compare the

requests of Jacob, Gen. 49:29-31; and Joseph, Gen. 50:25.) Is it important to you where you will be buried? What is your wish? Why?

_____

_____

_____

As I look back
As I look back, I see a story of faithfulness *[hesed], loyalty*. The main actor in chapter 24 is unnamed, but consistently called the "servant." He is a true and faithful servant of his master Abraham. This is service on the human plane; but through it, the servant also serves God, whom he humbly calls "Lord, God of my master Abraham." Nevertheless, this God is also his God; master and servant have equal access to him. The servant's mission was prompted by Abraham's own faithfulness shown in his effort not to allow the calling of God to be lost through acculturation to the Canaanites, or through a reversal of the way which God had led him.

Finally, it is the story of faithfulness of Rebekah and her family, shown in their compliance with God's leading once they have recognized it as such.

That leading is the second great impression left on me by the story of chapter 24. On the surface, that story moves along according to the dynamics of cause and effect. No unusual interference by God, no vision, no dream, no angel, no voice from heaven breaks into the commonplace chain of events. And yet, in all its earthiness, it is a deeply spiritual story, marked by the leading of God. None of the participants could have proved to a skeptical bystander that more than chance was at work. But to the persons involved, a pattern of events fell into place that was readily understood as the result of a gracious higher will. In this respect, the story is a model of what it means to live life in faith.

For us, the request of the servant for a sign may pose some questions. Ought we to find God's will in this way, too? Can one simply impose one's wish for certainty on God? Definitely not. God is not subject to any conditions we place on God. But sometimes, driven by true faith in God's grace that gives even what we have no right to claim, we may well stretch out our hand for an extra gift, as long as we leave it fully to God as to whether he will give it, or not. And at times, God does grant a sign, as many believers throughout history have testified.

As I look back, I also enjoy a story of singular tenderness and beauty. The old man and the young girl both serve, the one through his lifelong loyalty to his master, the other through her quick readiness to run with her jar for a stranger.

To conclude our reflection, and our study of the life of Abraham, we can do no better than to reread 25:7-11. If we have done our study attentively and well, we will sense the pathos that breathes through these verses. With restrained but deep emotion the writer takes leave of the most impressive and lovable figure in Genesis. He records his high age. He affirms the goodness and fullness of his life. He acknowledges both his sons, the natural as well as the elect. He underscores the important location of the burial, in the land of promise. He highlights the togetherness of husband and wife, partners in life and in death. And he notes that the promised son lives as blessed, near the "Well of the One Who Sees."

Faith and Life Bible Studies

Each one of the Faith and Life Bible Studies offers the student of the Bible a simple and straightforward way to study a book of the Bible or a portion of Scripture. The study process is designed to encourage a careful reading of the Bible and an application of the text to our time.

Books available from Faith and Life Bible Studies are:

Old Testament

Genesis 12—25: By Faith Abraham and Sarah by Waldemar Janzen
Micah: Better Than Rivers of Oil by Gerald Gerbrandt

New Testament

First Corinthians 1—7: Have the Mind of Christ by Marilyn Peters Kliewer
Colossians: Living as God's Chosen People by Helmut Harder
First Peter: Faith Refined by Fire by David Schroeder
Revelation: New Heaven on a New Earth by Philip Bender
To be published in 1987: *First Corinthians 8—16* by Marilyn and Werner Kliewer